For Philip, with love

Also by Thérèse Corfiatis and published by Ginninderra Press

Seasons of the Soul	*2000*
Emissaries of Light	*2006*
Northern Lights	*2008*
Edge of Tranquillity	*2010*
The Boy Who Loved the Moon	*2012*
Moonlight Wine GP Poets	*2014*
A Thousand Birds were Singing Picaro Poets	*2015*
Handfuls of Promise	*2015*
House of Dreams	*2016*
Absence of Clouds	*2017*
With Opened Eyes Picaro Poets	*2018*
Breath & other Poems	*2020*
Wonderment GP Poets	*2022*
Bridge of Words (with Britta Stenberg)	*2023*
The Meeting GP Poets (Britta Stenberg)	*2023*
Solar System Oracles Picaro Poets	*2023*
Keeper of the Flames GP Poets	*2023*

Thérèse Corfiatis

Harbour in Me

Acknowledgements

The following poems have previously appeared in Ginninderra Press publications:
'a dream of kunanyi' in Mountain Secrets anthology
'Wonderment' in Wonderment, Pocket Poets
'Winter Storm Front' in Wild anthology
'Poets in Prison' in I Protest: Poems of Dissent anthology
'The First Magnolia' and 'Dragon Kite Flying' in With Opened Eyes, Picaro Poets
'Thoughts in a Café' in The Crow
'Memory of an Evening' in The Meeting, Pocket Poets
'The Blind Woman' in The Crow

I am thankful to Stephen Matthews, former owner of Ginninderra Press, for his unwavering support over the last two decades. His belief and encouragement in my work was life changing. Stephen died in September, 2024, after a long illness. May his legacy live on.

Much gratitude to Hazel Girolamo and Fay Forbes for their insights and ever-present friendship forged through our mutual love of writing.

First published 2025 by
GINNINDERRA PRESS
PO Box 2 Bentleigh 3204
ginninderrapress.com.au

Contents

Gordon River

West coast of Tasmania

How, I ask myself
can a river lay so still
a looking glass
reflecting sky and cloud
birds on the wing
stencilled, like cut-outs
upon water as smooth
as a sheet of paper?

Not a ripple
on its band of satiny green
but for the funnelling
of the boat's passage
forming a perfect 'v'
trees at the river's edge
hold breath
not wanting to break the spell

a dream of kunanyi

Mt Wellington, Hobart, Tasmania

to the top of ancient kunanyi i came
and sailed into the sky
i looked below and saw the sea
as birds went soaring by

from the top of ancient kunanyi i saw
a world so sweet and new
my heart beat fast in the dream i had
and filled with joy anew

at the top of ancient kunanyi i felt
my soul rise on the air
it went asearching for my god
who was silently waiting there

Through Longford, Hobart Bound

Between high hedges in country lanes
I drive beneath bright autumn skies
happiness sits on my shoulder
and sunshine in my eyes

What a joy it is to travel
what a joy to be alive
so thankful for this perfect day
with the sunshine in my eyes

Fields fly away like autumn leaves
distant hills rise up and sing
colours speak to highest heavens
it is such a soulful thing

Crows lift up flapping from the road
sheep and cattle grazing land
little towns lay out a welcome
like a friend extends a hand

Stone bridges ford rushing streams
sweet music flowing there to hear
tiny finches swoop and play
whistling songs to meet my ear

I pray the journey's safely done
hours slip by, as does the day
and when I reach my destination
these are the words my heart shall say

What a joy it is to travel

what a joy to be alive
so thankful for this perfect day
with the sunshine in my eyes

Winter Solstice

Pelican Point Sanctuary, St Helens

Pond, a glaze of still blue-green
cloud drift upon its stippled surface
a dappled damask cloth

Wings tilted at impossible angles
a wren swoops low
trails its tiny shadow over water
lifts up, droplets shaken off
and streaks arrow-like into tall reeds

Frogs call beneath a crescent moon
a sickle song of first faint stars
reaping sunset's tones
a pond transformed into molten gold

Venus burns so close, so bright
a finger could reach out and touch it
like a wingtip brushing water
or frog song chorusing the moon
its iridescent crescent low in the sky
a winter solstice wonder

Birds of Tasmania

Songbirds uplift the heart
birds of prey arrest it –
the cry of a hawk
mate-seeking, hunting
pierces the air with echoing calls

Tiny blue wrens and finches
tinkle sweet crescendos
in the space around them
embodiment of beauty
feathers flash like jewels in the sun
as they forage and feed

Green rosellas are the chatty type
largest of its species
bright of body and eye
inhabiting Tasmania and the Bass Strait Islands
they feed on berries, seeds and flowers
making nests in hollow logs
to raise their young

Swift parrots squawk in noisy flocks
have families in the island's summer
retreating to a mainland winter
two species of flowering eucalyptus trees
comprise their main diet
their lives sadly in peril, habitat threatened
close to extinction

Black forest ravens
formidable, large, weighty
possess a recognisable dirge-like call
deep, mournful
tree dwellers, sedentary
they feed on lizards, insects and roadkill
and never leave our island shores

Masked lapwings
wear bold yellow face-masks
look permanently worried
devoted parents, they raise chicks on the run
in odd places like sports ovals, footpaths
neighbourhood lawns
swooping unsuspecting intruders

Native hens are chubby road runners
flightless, tiny-winged
found nowhere else but Tasmania
fiercely territorial, they repel transgressors
shrieking like fire alarms
chicks in tow, run like speeding fluff balls
a diet of grasses, herbs, insects and fruit
keeps them vigorous
their bright red eyes shine like rubies

Yellow-tailed black cockatoos
magnificent, large, boisterous
loop across the sky in wailing mobs
impossible to ignore
heard before they are seen
their arrival announced long distance
they roost in large gum trees at night
wings, black silk banners, ruffle against green

Yellow-throated honeyeaters
love the island's orchards
feasting on fruit, nectar and insects
the female makes exquisite nests
tree-fern fibres, spider's webs and hair
pilfered from live animals
she feeds and cares for nestlings on her own

Wedge-tailed eagles majestic
large, lanky, great soaring wings
with deep-powered beats
circling, drifting, spiralling
often silent, but sometimes
a high, thin whistle claims the sky their kingdom

How many awe-filled hours
are bequeathed to us from birds?
They come from a shell knowing what to do
and how to do it –
one of the planet's self-sustaining marvels
a connection between heaven and earth
and in a sense, giver of our wings

Some of this content was researched from Bird Watching in
Tasmania Travel Guide.

Wonderment

rain and wind swept in
curtaining the sea
laying gentle hands
upon foreshore and tree

it travelled up the hill
its cargo softly spilled
upon the window panes
in spidery lace and rills

droplets formed patterns
of a language yet unknown
trickled down onto the sill
and spoke its watery name

alive with breath and movement
outside the green ferns bent
a frilly, long-armed dance
in praise of wonderment

Mysterious Things

rain falls hard
sheets of nails
pierce flat steel seas

silver light
cuts like swords
penetrating dark fat clouds

water unloads
columns spiralling
slate grey skies

forest lifts up
its thirsty battalions
slaked upon the hill

the world speaks to me
of wild mysterious things
over which I have no power

the world speaks to me
its many forms
revealing wonders without end

The Heaving Blue

I woke one morning to a heaving blue
the heaving blue of sea and sky
it shot me through with such colour and light
I fell to my knees with a feeble cry
and wondered if I could rise again

Its beauty and awe, its spirit and might
bid me rise and stand and dance in the light
I spun and laughed in the bright high air
till exhausted I sank and drowned in the blue
of the heaving world that lives in me

It lingered all day, deep into the night
walked with each breath till I lay to sleep
and dreamt of wild places
forests, stone, moss and lake
and it remains unabated till now

This heaving blue that lives in me

Trees

Trees have a purity of presence
more so when mirrored in water
glass-still, quiet as a sigh
branches reach out and up
a chronicle of form and purpose
nourishment, shelter, protection

Beneath the sanctuary of trees
we have gathered together
in ritual and prayer
happiness shared –
childhood games, family picnics
sweethearts entwined –
in joy and sadness
trees have witnessed it all

In the mighty forests
of our world's continents
thriving belts of green
enfold the earth like hands
holding unfathomable treasure

Forests are as beautiful below
as they are above
a system of roots and runners
creating progeny, preserving soil
cleansing air and retaining water
a web of interconnectedness

In them, in their trust
lays all future promise
of a planet in harmony
of hope for a new Eden

In Old English, 'tree' was named treow meaning tree, trust or promise.

The Seed

Longing
is the seed
a catalyst
for all that is born
of our own
inner dreaming

Clouds

Magical and marvellous
clouds never lose appeal
blooms, spires, clusters
parapets, banners
suspend within them
a place to dream

Clouds hypnotise –
from childhood into adulthood
our beach walk companions
and at night, moonlit
reveal blinking stars
interspersed
in the spaces between them
like pulsing white fire

Artistry inhabits their form
rain, lightning and thunder
sing their choruses
but at dawn and sunset
beautiful shapes and shifting colours
move within them like a song
illuminated by the sun
centre of all that is

Reverie

Just after dawn
the world shook me awake
light, breath and birdsong
edging into consciousness

Serene and cool
its shimmering spoke
of a day promising warmth to come

Paddocks leached dry
shift yellow stalks in the wind
grassy notes of music swell

Pale cloud spreads its ribbons
patterning sky's blue expanse
ocean flips and curls
around shoreline rocks

Peace like this
calms tendrils of restlessness
an inner coil unwinding
a breath exhaled for all the lost things
melancholy for people no longer here
shrivelled roots of ancestry
for innocence
for words unsaid that could have been spoken
for those that stung
yet set, in their wounding, a heart
on pathways to forgiveness

Black cockatoos sail into vision
yellow tails flashing
screeching like banshees
interrupting thought –
rending cries diminish
as distance lengthens between us

I look up –
a white half moon sails
like a rose petal
suspended in the sky

With faith, nothing is lost
the banshee's wailing is simply noise
evaporating into space

Peace flickers at the wind's edges
pale cloud continues
to stream across the sky

Ocean's gentle drumming
its permanence
centres me
in a tune only I can hear

Bonds of Time

In the space between the trees
birds fly
clouds pass

In the space between the trees
shifting light and shadow
invokes a sense of freedom
a doorway to stillness
and at night
stars wheel a dance, so bright
our eyes lift up towards them
every breath a wonder

Days begin and end
as do all things for us

But in the depths of voyaging galaxies
bonds of time are slipped
ancestors walk eternity
existence and memory
merge with the present
a residue of their every action and thought
abides in us
vibrant with energy

Harbour in Me

Grey wild seas
slip sideways to the coast
tubular waves tumble
sandy shores rumble
shape, movement, sound
beautiful to see

These are moments
of feeling risen up
communion, not disconnection, the key
no sweeter thing could ever be

Grey wild seas
melt into grey wild skies
both consume each other
shifting this way and that
to find harbour in me

Port Augusta to Crystal Brook

A sense of ancient time
landscape evolved over aeons
red earth
pale grey-green scrub
luminous light
the bus trip secondary to all else

The Flinders Ranges
folds in and upon itself
soft whipped peaks of stone
mauve, russet, lavender
levitate above the earth
an exposed backbone

Another feeling overlays the first
the ranges seem composed
of a million vibrations
people's walking trails and songs
fashioning them into a purposeful form
where life played out its course
beneath a canopy of streaming stars

Cloud Consonants

Clouds materialise like consonants
clusters of altocumulus
nestle above horizons
wind breathes out d's and c's and b's

I try my best to decipher them
as sentences scroll before me
hundreds of words
elusive and tantalising

They scurry across the sky
disappearing then re-forming
into a new language
just out of reach

Sometimes I sit too long
vigilant, eyes heavy-lidded
weary from watching
I cannot look away

Protest Poets in Prison

may we learn to love as effortlessly
as light falling into sea

may we walk in goodness
breathe in hope, breathe out kindness
a force for change, for all that lives
upon earth, the air and sea

may we fall into oneness
may truth-seekers be heroes once again
generating energy and passion
for every soul seeking a dream

protest hatred, protest division
protest war and poets in prison
protest hunger, protest poisoned land
keep on protesting until we understand

how to love each other as effortlessly
as light falling into sea

Freedom's Song

Guards stare hard
march us up, march us down
no respite from fear's deep reign
we stand in line
with trembling knees
it's so very cold
this time of year

Orders barked out
we're told to keep still
slight swaying
perceived down the line
someone has cracked
and is starting to hum
it helps cast away all my fear

I start to join in
I don't care any more
I shuffle about in the line
I must be progressing
I continue to sing
maybe
for the very last time

The 46th President

He shuffles to the podium
a leader of the free world
struggling to remember
what he needs to say

A parody of himself
a grin, maybe confusion
spreads across his face
words tumble in disarray

The 46th president of the USA
frail, sometimes uncertain
offers no confidence
to those gathered nearby

This man is an instigator
part of a huge war machine
his family prospers
while countless people die

If we say and do nothing
the shadow of his axe
will fall on our heads
long before the downward sweep

It will be too late to weep
too late to flee
too late for a world
believing it was free

Do Not Forget the Flowers that Bloomed

Anzac Day 25/04/23

Do not forget the flowers that bloomed
bright and fresh and standing tall
a time when once the earth
was a garden for us all

Do not forget those homeland soils
where seeds were sown with love and care
and how such beauty shone when grown
to be uprooted, crushed by war

Do not forget the flowers that bloomed

Dance of the Checkpoints

Gaza Strip

and so, the dance of checkpoints begin
cars wait in long lines for hours
soldiers menacing
who dares defy
authority's face pressing in?

vehicles searched
people ordered out
belongings rifled, thrown aside

a pregnant woman waits
in summer heat
off-hand glances cast her way

she stands like a queen
oblivious it seems
to the chaos everywhere
hands clasp her belly
wherein grows all hope
of a people's future dreams

pity the people with no voice
with no rights
with no land to call their own

pity the children spurned at birth
by a world
that says it knows right from wrong

and the dance of the checkpoints
goes on and on
as the cars
wait
    in
      lines
          for
             hours

How to Start a Revolution

There is nothing like injustice
to start a revolution

Live well, love well
for each other, with each other

Take from this planet
return what it needs
keep all things in balance
a legacy of light
to shine in our children's eyes

This is the only way
to turn injustice on its heel

Disband armies
destroy guns, ammunition
melt down tanks
war planes, missile launchers
practise wholesome science
walk softly upon earth, all its places
unimpeded, unafraid

We inhabit an angry world
the gulf between need and greed widens

Stop the revolution before it begins

Bare Fist Fighter

Battered fists reveal the fight's fury
bruised and bleeding fingers
knuckles raw, reddened
breath comes hard

Above those fists
darts a dancer's eyes
the brain of a strategist
a knowing smile

Sometimes there is
no other way
words futile
pleas for reason, senseless

Sometimes a man must fight
for what he knows is right
to protect himself or others
may he stand tall

November Fourth

Hungarian day of national mourning for freedom fighters of the
1956 Revolution against the Soviet Union

At dusk
low in the sky's dimming light
a meteor slid across the heavens
it shed a smoky trail
and disappeared from sight

It brought to mind
a day of mourning
in a country far away
lives snuffed out like candle flames
cut down in freedom's name

Such courage
a beacon to the free world
people crushed under oppression's might
not lost in time, not lost in vain
for with perseverance they rose again

The Hungarian flag with a hole in its middle
became a symbol of a nation's hope
my grandmother prayed with hands on heart
prayers answered, long after her death
as the Iron Curtain gradually ripped apart
leading to the fall of the Berlin Wall

Descendants of the seven founding tribes
carry Magyar hearts bursting with pride
they stand as they have always stood
never bending the knee
but in brotherhood

Nem, nem, soha!*

Three words meaning free

* Nem, nem, soha: Magyar, meaning 'No, no, never!'

St Patrick's Day – Irish Blood

Our souls lay broken
ground down
from centuries of pain
shards and jagged edges
beneath the fall of every foot

Where are our healers
with their prayers, herbs and power
to make us whole again?

Our souls lay broken
reflecting glimpses
of sunlit fields and holy trees
villages held within earth's folds
rhythms of windswept shores
craggy coastline and island screes

Our souls lay broken
yet in our songs we remember
all that we are
a resonance, a strength
a deep and ancient pride
for all our Irish, near and far

Little Wrens and Nuclear Nightmares

It's an icy winter morning
little wrens forage in the garden
brilliant males flit vibrant blues over green grass
and into shrubbery

Ah, to be a bird, to live each day
without the heaviness we carry –
hunger, illness, mortgage stress, infidelity
violence, anger, homelessness
all quantified in varying degrees
by where a person lives on the planet –
little wrens are free of all these cares

I cannot imagine a world without little wrens
but lately thoughts sometimes turn
to doomsday scenarios
a legacy of my Hungarian father's deep distrust
of the former Soviet Union
seeping into my five-year-old consciousness –
such things mark a child
like a tattooed number on an arm

We know the script before its written
the roll-call of recent wars
Afghanistan, Korea, Vietnam, Cambodia
Egypt, Israel, Yugoslavia, Iraq, Iran
Lebanon, Syria, Ukraine, Russia
global conflicts played over and over
like a horror movie never losing its grim appeal

A winter fog rolls in
exacerbating gloomy thoughts
I feel caught
in some grey netherworld –
imagining terrible devastation
heralded by a nuclear cloud
billowing like a mushroom
shot through with lightning bolts, fiery flashes
a toxic sky, sea and wind

Ah, little wren
could you and your tiny troupe
survive the melted, twisted cities
ruined towns
breakdown of habitat
skeletal forests, poisoned earth?

Life in the twenty-first century
seems tenuous, fragile
held to ransom by the powerful few

Artificial intelligence, social media
alters the way our future beckons –
it holds within it a violence, vice-like
tentacles structured
to reach out and proclaim certain values as normal
such as one group of people
being superior to another
and in their superiority (itself a form of violence)
justify what they do
and how they do it

If we listen to the canary in the coal mine
or to blue wrens singing in the garden
maybe our children and their little ones
can know the beauty of a clear winter morning
and not be afraid of the impending fog

Ocean Waltz

clouds burst apart
like petalled flowers
sunlight strikes sea

flurries of skirted waves
lift up their hems
conducted by unseen hands

Awaiting Spring

On the brow of the hill
poplars stand still
morning mist rolls cold breath off the river

Bare trees hold empty nests like cups
woven whirls of twigs, feathers, grasses
fashioned by tiny beaks
such cleverness in those labours
an organic melding of inanimate into animate
a soft warm space for little eggs

A clump of daffodils call out to spring
pale sunlight speaks to the life within

Beside the river
mist transfigures
thin wispy trails fade into trees

The First Magnolia

Magnolia, unopened –
a polished pink pod
almost translucent
separate from tree
a pale, contained flame
shot through with sun,
unaware
of its own perfection

The flower
sits singular
on tapered stem
sprung up like a jewel,
blue-skied backdrop
accentuates fragility,
it appears
to levitate on air

Hypnotic
like the evening star,
its solitary beauty
shall soon be multiplied
in a rush
of clustered flowers
declaring
undeniable evidence of spring

Silver Gull Rites

As is their custom
in early evening
silver gulls soar
gliding back and forth
by the ocean's edge
as if to say
my beloved sea
I'll never leave you

As night approaches
they turn landwards
wheeling towards river banks
of soft green grass
or sandy stretches by the coast
to roost and rest

Do they dream in sleep
of gliding high above the ocean's face
feeling sunlight upon wings
of soft watery hands
holding buoyant bodies?

Every morning
a search for sustenance begins
they stamp feet, imitating rain
luring food to hungry beaks
mothers tend their young

They live and congregate
in great colonies
intelligent, curious
possessing hardy bodies, sharp eyes
learning from collective experience
how to exist with each other
and with us

Good parents
they teach squawking younglings
what it is to be a gull
and like those of us with mates
remain true to each other
a bonded pair living twenty years and more

They protect each other
by flashing signals with their wings
semaphore for birds
and those very wings
through each and every season
dive and soar and swoop
aerial gymnastics displaying the art of flight

Loud and clear
their cries are haunting
and those who hear them
by a windswept shore
or beneath a moonlit sky
will stop and listen
and understand, for a moment
what it is to be free

Autumn Starlings and First Stars

dusk lingers
amber cloud
paints velvet skies
like no other

autumn nestles in
covering itself
in blankets
of bright leaves

gum trees
stand reflected
by a river
in stasis

starlings perch
on power lines
like notes of music
heads bent in chatter

they fly off
regroup
settle themselves
tittering softly

wind lifts
river stipples
starlings fall silent
first stars faintly shine

Winter Storm Front

North-west Tasmania

Icy Antarctic blasts
sweep across the island
tress bent, an agony of twisted limbs
swirling leaves jettisoned on air
birds shriek out alarms
clawing, clinging to footholds

All melds into a frenzy
senses confused
colours, sounds, smells overlap

Ocean churns and froths
erupting against the sky
as horizontal rain slants in
whipping along streets
roofs clattering
a million cutting knives

Heavy clouds of dark grey sails
fill the sky
rudderless, surging forwards
an armada threatening
no quarter given in any direction

Orange Blossom Words

rain and wind swirls
orange blossoms fall
settling beneath trees
like words finding a soft place
patiently awaiting thought
to resurrect them

The Garden at Seaford

For Peter

Magpies, most magnificent, strut and sing
they too enjoy the garden's shade and layered green
a birdbath for happy splashing
its pool reflecting sky and cloud

Thoughts resurface of other gardens –
my grandmother's apricots, plums, strawberries
fat green runner beans –
a sister's Adelaide garden
native plants, almond trees, possums, crows
a pond for fish and waterlilies

Another sister's Hobart garden
crammed full of flowers
cool climate shrubs
herb beds, vegie patch
stone pagodas, wind chimes, a swing seat –
all three gardens beautiful
tended with love
places of purpose, peace, tranquillity

In daylight
the Seaford garden beckons
rosemary bushes spread scented grasping arms
upwards along windows
fingers release oils to invigorate, refresh –
the garden quivers with produce and life
things to be eaten, cooked and savoured
a sheen to everything that grows
under the sun

In moonlight
the garden brims with shadows
memories, silence and meditation –
in rain, a gloss and glisten
to each leaf, stem, flower
stamen, bud, thorn, rock –
the smell of sweet damp earth
hovering like holy incense
impregnating root systems
promising abundance

One morning I woke to creeping light
birdsong echoing through vast halls of air and trees
the garden by my window a blessing
its structure, placement, colour
infusing delight

I glimpsed, almost by accident
its guardian, kneeling in silence
surveying his kingdom
his body bent forwards
in a state of grace and reverence
willing his vision to thrive

This, I shall carry home with me
like a benediction

Greenvale – Woodlands Historic Park

Victoria

Out in Greenvale
frogs are calling
magpies sing midnight notes

Streets are dark
everyone sleeps
stars sparkle above

Red river gums
gleam in moonlight
sentinels, tall and strong

In the distance
Melbourne city
highlights the skyline

Nature and people
collide with each other
suburban sprawl spreads

Songlines are silent
old ways forgotten
undercurrents of pain

A spider's web
quivers on air, portent
of future struggles

Pity the people
who once roamed here free
as shadows slip into the trees

Clouds over Suburbia

North of Melbourne

Houses resemble Lego sets
neat rows along footpaths
manicured gardens and lawns

New subdivisions spread out
earth cleared, trees razed –
infrastructure creeps along highways

Morning and evening
neighbours file in and out front doors
some wave a cheery hello

At local shopping centres
mothers wheel toddlers
juggling groceries, bottles and toys

Coles cashiers wear hijab
huge-eyed, black-lashed, soft-cheeked
patient, as the elderly count notes and coins

Family businesses thrive
polite, smiling, industrious folk
bilingual, eager to serve and please

Victoria's demographic changing
Arabic and Assyrian spoken everywhere
a fusion of cultures

Cloud rumbles, a late spring storm
charges across bulging skies
thunder cracks, heavy rain falls

People dash for shelter; a small finch
sings from a tall eucalyptus tree
others gather in sweet layers of song

Under cover, old men chat, smoke
while above, black crows call
sodden wings flap through the air

Below the sky's unfastened clouds
people and nature co-exist
often fragile, bound as one

Fractions of time
captured in moments
fellowship found in each other

A Three-year-old's Hands

For Alexander

His hands are always warm
soft, supple
beautiful fingers
prodding, probing, exploring
living antennae

He draws lines and swirls
forms letters of his own design
stacks blocks, pushes cars
paints deftly with downward strokes
can extricate one long hair
from his mamma's head
fallen upon the floor

He inspects smooth pebbles
delights in water
opens kitchen cupboards
navigates a laptop's icons
scrutinises a door's lower hinges
and picks dandelion heads

Sitting on dadda's lap
his little hands play the keyboard
gently hold his mamma's clothes
and when sleepy and tired at night
cuddle his favourite pussy cat pillow

On the day he was born
I held him against my heart
his tiny fingers clutched mine
and I wondered
what shall these little hands create
when he becomes a man?

Mother and Son

The little one watches the plane
roll to a halt on the tarmac

I point at it, saying

Mum's coming. Look.

Framed in dappled light
he spots her in its doorway –
a small cry of joy escapes him

Mamma.

We walk together to greet her

Squatting down
she holds him in the circle of her arms
his head upon her shoulder
weeks of longing dissolved

In the car
he clasps her hand tight
only relinquishing it when he arrives home

Layers

I asked my grandson

What did you do at school today?

No reply   He looks at me with serious eyes

Later, he scrolls through photos
on my mobile phone, and says

Boat Harbour beach

He's running barefoot
across wet sand
smiling, pink-cheeked, damp hair
he shines like an angel
encased in summer light

Behind him, a mound of craggy rocks
slashed with deep orange
dwarf him with their bulk

By the shoreline
stones are bevelled yellow
striped like sweets on a counter
two distinct layers of rock formation

His four-year-old life
leaps out of the image
in juxtaposition to a landscape
formed millions of years ago

I see in his human form
a moment captured in a photo
his existence
no less miraculous than a grain of sand

He's taken from this summer day
bright sunshine, ocean's touch
wind and salt
a sense of something far bigger than himself
much more than he could ever learn
within four walls of a classroom

I watch him engrossed in the photo
studying his flight along the beach
enjoyment, wonder, curiosity
play at the corners of his mouth
layers of memory resurface
his happiness recalled

Winter Drive – Isandula Road

North-west Tasmania

We drove into damp green forest
tall, spindly gums massed together
like Italian frescoes against sky's grey backdrop
my little grandson verbose
enthralled by the world
avid eyes darting everywhere

Small bridges traversed country creeks
bulging with stones
water, full of lace and froth
circumnavigates obstacles at high speed

Each bend of the road
each up and down
revealed new marvels –
huge ferns, fronds like windmills
tiny finches flitting together
no larger than a walnut
songs like miniature bells

Nearer to the coast
a more ordered landscape
farms, quaint houses, sheds and tractors –
to our left, high hills and mountains
to our right, valleys cutting downwards to the sea
animals in paddocks, tilled earth chocolate brown

Later that night I sat with him
he yawned and chattered, hard to settle –
I drifted off into the forest
his words gradually thinning out
rising high above the spindly treetops
as we both moved towards sleep

Autist Unsettled – Memories Resurface

Little grandson sleeps over
autist unsettled

Memories resurface
of his dad, my oldest son when small
needing time to defrag
a brain thrumming with obsessive details
trying to obscure fractured thoughts
his need for repetition necessary
a calming thing
floating its own boat
upon a sea of melting anxieties
circles of entanglement
decreasing in ever diminishing spheres
until they became a tiny dot
an entry point for his fall into darkness
into a blessed state of sleep

Memories resurface
of my youngest son as a five-year-old
his new black and white kitten
curled in the crook of his legs
his little hand reaching down to stroke its head
boy and kitten drifting into a gentle space
settling to rest

Memories resurface
this time of his anger
on hearing how teenagers
taunted his brother in the street
he wanted to smash them
defend him
protect him
deflect embarrassment
in an aggressive act of love

To travel our road
has not been easy
subjected to people's callousness
judgements, sneers, ignorance
words of pity

Projections of their own unease
always made us uneasy

Tonight when I lay down to sleep
I'll dream of my sons' preciousness
perform my rituals
upon the altar of their belonging
place flowers lovingly
on a golden cloth spun out of belief
as witness to my abiding hope
in all they strive for
and long to be

Autism's Cloud

Once upon a time
a cloud, full and bulbous
threatened rain, good rain
its dark, silver-lined form
holding water and life

In this century's time and space
a cloud can also mean data
a busyness of information gathered
social media a part of daily life
humanity barraged with floods of fact and fiction
a perfect environment for a neuro-diverse brain

I watch my son immersed in his computer
in his cloud
scrolling, stopping, reading
absorbed, inspired, informed

Before him sits a perfect ally
one who responds in an instant
one who neither confronts nor denies
one who brings knowledge
one who presents beautiful images
one who plays eclectic music

I ponder at all the data
clustering in his head
a million tiny clouds brimming
so full   so full
rain falling in endless streams of data
sprouting fresh promises of green tomorrows

Dragon Kite Flying

For Yousif

Up into the air
the kite soared
its dragon tail whipping wind
while far below
the boy's eyes followed its path
hands manipulating strings
brow furrowed in concentration

he allowed the kite to climb higher
then reeled it slowly in
happiness displayed
in a wide-mouthed grin
his mastery of flight and speed
a thing he could control
a domain to rule over

Fresh Things

crescent moon
hangs silver
dawn spreads
orange wings

light seeps
into sky
promising
fresh things

August Seventh

Days lengthen in August
light lingers longer
a month ushered in by storms
scudding cloud
luscious rain-swept skies
heads of hyacinth, daffodil, violet
announce new brilliance
offsetting washed grey spaces

on this day
my mother rises in me like a tide
swells me to my shore
I give thanks for her young body
and what it endured

she set me down in my cradle
like a little boat
rocked upon a sea of love

seven is my favourite number
the day of her birth
the number of people in my family
one for each day of the week

approaching my seventh decade
she walks my every journey
and I swear
if I turn to look behind me
she is there
an enigmatic smile
curving her beautiful mouth

Ashes Scattered For a Mother

Cascade Gardens, South Hobart
For David

He crouches
in the middle of the creek
feet positioned on islands of stone

head bowed, long dark hair
a cowl about his shoulders
hands firm around the urn

ashes pour downwards
slipping through light
like a breath inhaled from below

blending and swirling
we watch in silence
water wends them away

he kept some to scatter
beneath tall blackwood trees
guards of honour in a row

we laid stones of remembrance
upon the earth, wedged others
into rivulet's clefts

daughter, sister, wife, mother
from the place of your birth
in us, like a river you flow

home is a heart
grieving and grateful
where none of us travel alone

Siblings

It rankles
like an item of clothing
not fitting properly

I dream of us
knitted close
in a fabric of love

Sometimes
I am reminded of its friction
I fidget, smooth it down

I dream of us
nurturing
commonalities

It's only a temporary release
somehow
the cloth never sits right

Armchair's Lament

For Philip

He told me
how he sat in my empty chair
when I was away
looking out to an ocean
where I'd gaze and daydream
every day

He told me
the house
missed my presence

It's good to be home, I said

We smile at each other
and watch clouds
trail windblown patterns across the sky

All Clear

Recurring visits
by family members
to oncologists
punctuate life with anxiety

What is life without hope?

How often
have we heard this said
not really appreciating
its deeper meaning?

My husband
is a cancer survivor
how sweet the words
all clear

The longer we live
awareness grows
of what will come
it's inevitable
unstoppable
but we want old age
to settle about us
like warm scarves
around thin necks
comforting our skin

A Glass of Water

All our travels bore witness to water

Dubai's futuristic skyscrapers
surreal, lurched up from desert sands
sea-water desalinated for a city's needs
avenues of green palm, lush parks
swirling fountains with music and light
streams of tourists
visiting one of earth's driest cities

In Athens, Corinth, Olympia
tiny cups of coffee set down with water
and in Delphi
we drank from the Castalian Spring
regarded by the ancients
as a source of poetic inspiration

The Pythia and priests
cleansed themselves
before the Oracle spoke her prophecies
pilgrims quenched their thirst, as did we
held in thrall by a sanctuary
set high amongst mountains
sapphire skies with soaring eagles
the omphalos of the world

On Santorini
water seemed to materialise
out of thin air at night
moisture forming
a by-product
of the island's microclimate
a natural process akin to breathing

Budapest's water straight from a tap
sweet, clear, cold
drawn from subterranean sources
and pure water of Transylvania
a benediction to drink or bathe in
springs and wells dotted everywhere
mineral rich, strong to the taste

In Paris, Bordeaux, Istanbul, Rhodes
drinking fountains
mapped out a trail for thirsty mouths
through every adventure walked
and wondered at

Rivers and waterways
threaded land like veins in a body
shoreline marking boundaries
of continents and islands
until we flew across vast Australian deserts
flat, iron-coloured, empty
her first peoples carrying knowledge
of where to find precious water

It was then I understood
how water evokes recollection
and a sense of place

Arriving home
fatigued from long flights
our luggage stood unpacked in the hallway
I sat with a glass of water
raised it to my lips
and drank it down

my throat swallowed a thousand memories
and hoped for a thousand more to come

Sunset's Glow

Light reflected from winter skies
burnished houses facing west
and thought rolled backwards in time
drawing comparisons with Greek villages
springtime on beautiful Santorini
houses bathed in sunset's glow

I walked on into winter's twilight
these images held in my mind
thinking of people and places
and of how the same sun
sets on all mankind

Memory of a Finnish Lake

little wooden dinghy
bobs a tethered rhythm
lake as round as a coin
encircled by sun-struck forest

everything glimmers
birch trees shimmer
dragonflies whirr
waterlilies stir

a tiny jetty juts out
a broken tooth in an open mouth
children run
bare feet slapping boards

they spill from its edge
like a mouthful of crumbs
dispersed to water
not a duck in sight

Thoughts in a Café

They've been coming here
as have I
for years

A little more stooped
longer silences
quietly sipping lattes

I wonder
if they've noticed
the changes in me?

I am greyer
more hesitant
sagacious, softer

We smile at each other
kindness
our common envoy

Another year
fades slowly
just like us

Memory of an Evening

After supper we sat talking
watching the ocean's moods
and the thin orange cat
who lived somewhere on my street
appeared at the glass doors
wailing for company and food

I miss my Lily, she said –
her much loved ageing tabby
at the other end of the world
she must wonder where I am
I commented maybe cats
possess a different concept of time

She went outside
a backdrop of shifting sea and sky
framed them perfectly
sat to pet him, held him
spoke to him, as he looked up
with grateful golden eyes

Maybe he sensed her need
as he raised his face towards her
butted his head against her arms
a huge dose of cat love
enough, I hoped, to sustain her
until she returned home

Notes to my Deceased Cat, Boysie

Boysie, a few years on
lizards scurry freely
explore garden beds
sunbathe on upturned stones
warm themselves
by the wide back doorstep

Small, fat, thin, long
they appear more frequently
no longer driven
to dash for grassy hiding places
cracks in the path
or to relinquish tails

I miss you cat
my chatty, bright-eyed
ever observant friend
but as lizards lounge and linger
it seems all memory of you
has passed into reptilian legend

The Blind Woman

she walks with a cane
at its tip a small white ball rolls
her personal gps navigator

she steps confidently
hair streaming in the wind
like the wake of a little boat

she makes her way
one footfall after another
like two stones placed in a wall

knowing not
the length and breadth and height
of that which they are a part of

Writing Letters

For Maureen

Loops and dots and swirls
embellish the page
thoughts captured
in deep concentration
pivot on the person I am writing to
pondering how to convey
my present reality

Destined to travel
via air, sea and land
my words hibernate in an envelope
by the time she receives it
my actual reality will be altered
having slipped into the past
to become part of her current day

I picture her studious face
reading my letter
weighing my life in her hands
and I wait for a reply
capturing her reality
posted to me
arriving backwards in time

www.ingramcontent.com/pod-product-compliance
Lightning Source LLC
Chambersburg PA
CBHW071246020426
42333CB00015B/1648